CHECKERBOARD NATURE LIBRARY

INSECTS

Crickets

by Cari Meister

ABDO
Publishing Company

visit us at
www.abdopub.com

Published by ABDO Publishing Company, 4940 Viking Drive, Suite 622, Edina, Minnesota 55435. Copyright © 2001 Abdo Consulting Group, Inc., Pentagon Tower, P.O. Box 36036, Minneapolis, Minnesota 55435 USA. International copyrights reserved in all countries. No part of this book may be reproduced in any form without written permission from the publisher.

Printed in the United States

Illustrators: Edwin Beylerian, Carey Molter

Cover photo: Corbis Images

Interior photos: Animals Animals, Artville, Corel, Corbis Images, Digital Vision, John Foxx Images, Peter Arnold, Inc., PhotoDisc, PictureQuest

Editors: Tamara L. Britton, Kate A. Furlong

Design and production: MacLean & Tuminelly

Library of Congress Cataloging-in-Publication Data

Meister, Cari.
   Crickets / Cari Meister.
      p. cm. -- (Insects)
   ISBN 1-57765-460-9
    1. Crickets--Juvenile literature. [1. Crickets.] I. Title.

QL508.G8 M45 2000
595.7'26--dc21

                                       00-056889

Contents

What is a Cricket?

Crickets live all over the world. There are more than 2,600 kinds of crickets. Some crickets are less than one inch (2.5 cm) long. But, others are more than two inches (five cm) long.

Crickets and their close relatives—grasshoppers and katydids—make beautiful music. In many countries, people keep crickets as pets. That way, they can enjoy the cricket's chirping sound. Male crickets chirp the most, but sometimes females chirp, too. Male crickets chirp louder than females. Crickets chirp for many reasons. Male crickets chirp to attract female crickets, and to scare other males away. A cricket may also chirp to warn other crickets that danger is near.

Tree cricket.

Some crickets are brightly colored.

Katydids are closely related to crickets.

The Cricket's Body

A cricket's body is divided into three main sections. They are the head, thorax, and abdomen. The head is the first part, the thorax is the middle part, and the abdomen is the last part.

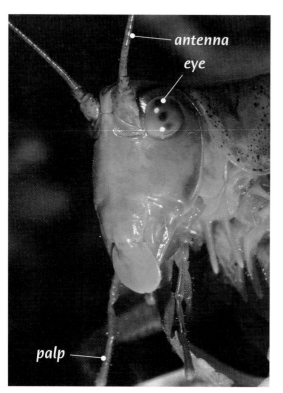

antenna

eye

palp

On a cricket's head are its **compound eyes**. Between the compound eyes are three **simple eyes**. Near the cricket's mouth are **palps**.

Above the cricket's eyes are two large antennae. The cricket's antennae are sense organs. Using its antennae, a cricket can tell if the air is dry or humid. The antennae can sense sounds and smells, too.

6

On the cricket's thorax are four wings. Crickets have special parts on their front wings to chirp. On one wing is the file and on the other is the scraper. When the cricket rubs the file against the scraper, it makes chirping sounds. A special **membrane** called the mirror near the file and scraper makes the chirp sound louder.

Inside the abdomen, there are muscles for flying and jumping. There is a gut to digest food. There are organs for mating. There is a heart to pump blood. Crickets do not have red blood, like you. Most crickets have white or yellowish blood.

Many crickets have feelers, called cerci, on the end of their abdomens. The cerci allow a cricket to feel its way around in the dark.

Crickets have very strong legs. They are good jumpers. Crickets have ear slits on their front legs!

Crickets do not have skeletons on the inside of their bodies. They have **exoskeletons**. As a young cricket grows, it sheds its exoskeleton many times. Sometimes crickets eat their old exoskeleton.

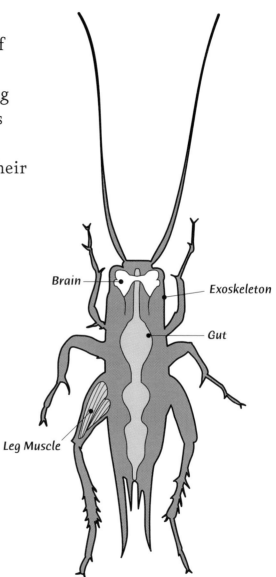

Brain

Exoskeleton

Gut

Leg Muscle

How They Grow

Crickets have three life stages. They are egg, nymph, and adult. After a female mates, she gets ready to lay her eggs. She digs a hole in damp sand. She digs with a special tube on the back of her abdomen called an **ovipositor**. Then the cricket lays her eggs in the holes she dug.

A provence cricket lays an egg sack on a thistle.

When the eggs hatch, nymphs wiggle out. Nymphs look like adult crickets. But, they do not have all of the adult body parts yet. Nymphs eat a lot and grow fast. As they grow, they **molt**. Nymphs molt several times. After each molt, they look more like adult crickets.

Cricket nymph.

Cricket molting.

What They Eat

Different kinds of crickets eat different kinds of food. Some crickets only eat plants. Some crickets eat plants and animals. When crickets eat, their jaws move sideways.

What kind of food a cricket eats depends on what kinds of mouthparts it has. House crickets eat almost anything. They have special jaws that smash up all kinds of food. Mole crickets eat roots and seedlings.

This cricket is eating pollen from a flower.

Mole cricket.

Where They Live

Crickets live all over the world. They live in the **savannas** of Africa. They live in the wet, dark woods of Europe. They live in the gardens of Australia. They may even live in your backyard.

Many kinds of crickets live in wooded or grassy areas. Some crickets only live in hot, dry places.

The mole cricket lives underground. It has special thick front legs. The sturdy legs are good for digging. Mole crickets build tunnels underground. They rarely come up to the surface.

Mole cricket.

The most common kind of cricket is the field cricket.
Field crickets live in meadows and weeds all over the world.
The house cricket prefers to live indoors.

Field cricket.

Enemies

Many animals like to eat crickets. Cats, lizards, frogs, snakes, and skunks all eat crickets. Some animals, including some insects, like to eat cricket eggs.

Crickets protect themselves from their enemies in several ways. They hop away. They fly away. They also hide under rocks, sticks, and in deep grass.

Lizard eating a cricket.

Many crickets blend into their surroundings. This is called camouflage. For example, Jerusalem crickets are brown with black stripes. They live on rocky hillsides. The pebbles on the hillsides are also brown and black. This makes the Jerusalem cricket hard to see.

Jerusalem cricket.

Night tree cricket.

Many crickets are nocturnal. Night is a safer time for crickets to hunt and mate than during the day. It is easier to hide in the dark.

Crickets & People

Most crickets are not harmful. In fact, many people keep crickets as pets. Crickets are easy to keep. They do not need to be walked. They do not eat much and they make wonderful music. Crickets are often kept in special cages, like songbirds.

Some kinds of crickets help keep pests out of apple orchards. Insect larvae eat apples. Crickets eat insect larvae. Crickets are a natural way to get rid of the apple pests. Using crickets is better for the environment than spraying **pesticides**.

Crickets eat pests that hurt apple trees.

Very few crickets are harmful. But, some crickets can cause damage. Mole crickets build underground tunnels. As they burrow, they rip up grass and plant roots. And, house crickets sometimes eat clothes.

Mole cricket.

House cricket.

Fun Facts

🦗 Crickets chirp faster when it is warmer. The colder it gets, the less they chirp.

🦗 Cave crickets have antennae that are sometimes twice as long as their bodies! These long antennae help them find their way inside dark caves.

🦗 Some crickets, like the Eastern ant cricket, live in ant nests. They have a very unusual way of getting food. They tickle an ant's abdomen until the ant throws up its food, then they feast!

Cave cricket.

20

Male crickets are awesome fighters. If a male cricket invades another male cricket's territory or tries to take its food, the cricket will use its strong jaws to try and bite its enemy to death.

Close-up of a cricket's head.

Glossary

camouflage – to conceal; to blend into the surroundings.

compound eyes – eyes that have many small lenses.

exoskeleton – the outer casing that protects an insect.

membrane – a thin layer of tissue.

molt – to shed old skin and replace it with new skin.

mouthparts – a structure near the mouth that an insect uses to eat.

nocturnal – when an animal is active at night.

ovipositor – a female cricket's egg-laying tube.

palps – sense organs.

pesticides – something (like a chemical) used to destroy pests; many pesticides are harmful to the environment.

savanna – a treeless plain.

simple eyes – eyes with only one lens.

Web Sites

http://www.ex.ac.uk/bugclub/

Join the Bug Club! This site for young entomologists includes a newsletter, puzzles, and games.

http://www.insecta.com

This site hosted by the University of British Columbia has great information on all kinds of bugs. Read about the bug of the month, listen to great bug sounds, and look at a bug family tree!

Index